My Life in Recipes

Compiled by:

Jessica Joy Tipler

Dedicated to the plethora of family, friends and foes that have inspired my life through cooking.

A special thank you to Colette Holton, Susan Tipler and many others for the use of your recipes or adaptations of your recipes.

Nature's 12 Great Protectors

This list is on the first page of my tattered paper cookbook, and it reminds me to try to incorporate these and other healthy foods into my diet every day.

Your best defense against free radicals:

Grape juice
Kale
Prunes
Spinach
Strawberries
Blueberries
Beets
Oranges
Cranberry juice
Red peppers
Cherries
Green tea

Table of Contents

Chocolate avocado
pudding
Chocolate chip cookies
Chocolate icing
Cream cheese icing
Crème Brulée
Dee's donuts
Gingerbread cake
Gingerbread cookies
Gingersnaps
Grammy's frozen
mold
Haystacks
Ice cream
Iron skillet apple pie
Key lime pie
Key lime pie – Holton
family recipe

Lemon cream cheese
cookies
Lemon snow bars
Lunchroom brownies
Peanut butter cookies
Pecan Pie
Pecan rolls
Pie crust
Poppyseed cake
Pound cake
Pumpkin crisp
Pumpkin pie
Ricotta cake
Rum cake
Sand tarts
Silver moon chocolate
chip cookies
Sugar cookies

Drinks/Cocktails, page 149
Blue Hawaii
Bucky's mint julep
Chai tea
Lychee cocktails
Mojito
St. Germaine cocktail

BREAKFAST

7-up Bisquick Biscuits

Ingredients:
4 cups Bisquick
1 cup sour cream
1 cup 7-up or Sprite
½ cup melted butter

Preheat oven to 425 degrees. Melt butter in cast iron. Mix all ingredients, roll out and cut into biscuits. Put in melted butter. Bake for 15 minutes or so.
*I usually half recipe and it yields about 8 biscuits.

Apple Oatmeal Muffins
Recipe from my mom, Colette Holton

Ingredients:
1 cup all-purpose flour
3 tsp baking powder
½ tsp. salt
½ cup sugar
¼ cup brown sugar
1 cup Quaker Oats
1 cup diced apples
1 egg, beaten
½ cup milk
1 tsp cinnamon

Preheat oven to 400 degrees. Combine the flour, baking powder and salt. Add the sugar, brown sugar, Quaker Oats, apple, beaten egg, milk and cinnamon. Mix well. Place in a greased muffin pan. Bake for 10-15 minutes. You can top with 1 Tbsp of sugar and 1 tsp. cinnamon before baking, but it isn't essential.

Banana Bread
Recipe from my mom, Colette Holton

Ingredients:
1 stick of softened butter
1 cup sugar
2 eggs (beaten)
2 cups all-purpose flour
2 tsp. salt
1 tsp. baking soda
3-4 ripe bananas

Preheat oven to 350 degrees. Grease a loaf pan. Blend together butter and sugar. Add the beaten eggs. Combine the remainder of the dry ingredients and add them to the butter mixture. Mash 3-4 ripe bananas. Add to the other ingredients. Mix well. Place in the loaf pan and bake for 1 hour.

Biscuits
Recipe from my mom, Colette Holton

Ingredients:
2 cups self-rising flour
1 tsp salt
1 stick butter, refrigerated and cut into pea size pieces
1 cup milk

Preheat oven to 400 degrees. Combine the flour and salt. Stir in butter and milk. Mix until all flour is wet. If too sticky, add a little more flour. Roll or pat out dough to 1" thick on floured surface. Cut out biscuits with a biscuit cutter or the top of a glass cup. Bake for 10-12 minutes. Yields six biscuits.

Cinnamon Rolls
Recipe from Andrew's Grandmom, Betty Mullins

Ingredients:
1 container of refrigerated crescent rolls
Butter
Sugar
Cinnamon

Preheat oven to 375 degrees. Unroll the crescent rolls.
Working one by one, place unrolled roll on a cookie sheet.
Place 2 pats of butter and heavily dust with sugar and
cinnamon. Roll up and repeat until you have all of the rolls on
the pan. Bake for 15 minutes or until desired doneness.

Maple Brown Sugar Bacon
Andrew's mouthwatering recipe

Ingredients:
8-10 strips of nice, thick bacon
2 Tbsp brown sugar
2 Tbsp maple syrup
pinch cayenne pepper (if you want it to have a kick)

Preheat oven to 400 degrees. Combine the brown sugar with the cayenne (if using cayenne). Place the bacon on a rack on a baking sheet. Brush the bacon with maple syrup. Sprinkle the brown sugar mixture over the bacon. Bake in the preheated oven until desired doneness, typically 12-20 minutes, but it just depends.

One Eyed Joe

Recipe inspired by my father in-law, Steve Tipler

Ingredients:
Sliced bread
Butter
Eggs
Salt and pepper

Melt a tsp of butter in a non-stick pan over medium high heat. Place your bread on the cutting board and cut out a circle in the center with a biscuit cutter. Toast the hole and the bread with the hole in it in the melted butter. Once nearly toasted on one side, crack an egg and pour the egg into the hole of the toast. Sprinkle with salt and pepper. Flip after about 1 minute. Finish cooking on the other side to your desired doneness.

Pancakes

Ingredients:
1 ½ cups all-purpose flour
3 ½ tsp baking powder
1 tsp salt
1 Tbsp white sugar
1 egg
1 ¼ cups milk
3 Tbsp melted butter

Mix dry ingredients together. Make a well in the center of the dry mix and pour in the milk, egg, and melted butter. Mix until smooth. Cook on a lightly oiled griddle ¼ - ½ cup per pancake.

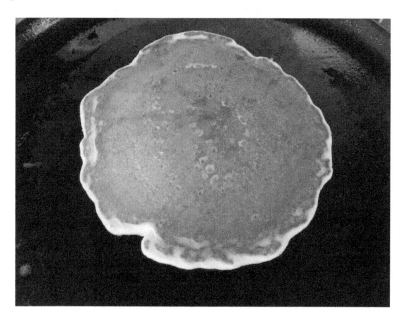

Potato Pancakes
Recipe from John Campbell

Ingredients:
3-4 strips of bacon
¼ cup red onion
1 cup bread flour
1 cup potato flakes
¼ cup shredded Manchego cheese
2 pinches baking powder
Salt and pepper to taste
2 tomatoes
Oil for cooking
Milk to consistency (about 1 cup)

Brown bacon and remove. Sauté shredded onion in bacon fat. Remove. Remove. Mix together flour, potato flakes, baking powder, cheese, onions, browned bacon chips, salt, pepper and milk. Heat oil over medium heat. Divide potato mixture into three 1-2" flat disks. Cook on both sides until brown. Serve with tomatoes on top.
*Okra is a good side dish for this.

Vegan Spelt Muffins
From Jenny at the Camaraderie Café

Ingredients:
1 2/3 cup spelt
½ tsp baking powder
¼ tsp baking soda
½ tsp cinnamon
¼ tsp salt
Fruit or chocolate chips
*dried coconut for the topping

Mix all dry ingredients and then add:

1 tsp vanilla extract
1 oz apple sauce
3 oz soy milk
2 oz oil
4 oz maple syrup

Preheat oven to 350 degrees. Spoon into muffin pan and top with the dried coconut, if desired. Bake at 350 degrees for 5 minutes. Reduce heat to 325 degrees and bake for 35-45 minutes (if making mini muffins, cook the first five minutes at 350 and then 12 minutes at 325)

Waffles

Ingredients:
3 Tbsp melted butter
1 ½ cup flour
1 ½ tsp baking powder
Pinch of salt
2 Tbsp sugar
1 ½ cup milk
2 eggs

Melt the butter. Preheat the waffle iron. Combine the dry ingredients. Combine the wet ingredients, excluding the butter. Combine both mixtures. Add the melted butter. Use the waffle iron to cook about 1/3 cup of mixture at a time. (Recipe makes about five waffles in standard iron)

SOUPS/SAUCES

2-Hour Pork Chop Brine

Ingredients:
¾ cups Kosher salt
1 cup brown sugar
1 Tbsp black peppercorns
1 Tbsp mustard powder
2 cups apple cider vinegar
1 lb ice cubes
Up to five pork chops

Heat vinegar, salt, sugar, peppercorns, mustard in a large pot. Allow to get hot enough for salt and sugar to dissolve.

Let cool for 20 minutes. Put in a container with ice cubes. Add the pork chops and put them in the refrigerator for no more than two hours. Rinse them off and they are ready to cook or can be held until needed.

Basic White Sauce
Recipe from Leia Hamlyn

Ingredients:
2 Tbsp melted butter
2 Tbsp all-purpose flour, sifted
¼ tsp salt
1 cup milk
Black pepper to taste

In a small pot, melt butter and stir in the flour. Cook for approximately one minute. Whisk in the milk. Bring the mixture to a boil. Reduce heat. Add salt and black pepper.

Caribbean Potato Soup

Ingredients:
2 medium onions, chopped
2 tsp oil
3 garlic cloves, minced
2 tsp fresh ginger, minced
2 tsp ground coriander
1 tsp ground turmeric
½ tsp dried thyme
¼ tsp ground allspice
1 tsp salt
5 cups chicken stock
2 cups cubed, peeled sweet potatoes
3 cups fresh kale, chopped
1 cup fresh or frozen okra
1 cup coconut milk
1 cup canned diced tomatoes, drained
1 cup canned black eyed peas, rinsed and drained
2 Tbsp lime juice

In a Dutch oven, sauté onions in oil until tender. Add the garlic, ginger, and spices. Cook one minute longer. Stir in broth and potato. Bring to a boil. Reduce heat. Cover and simmer five minutes longer. Stir in kale and okra. Return to a boil. Cover and simmer 10 minutes longer or until potato is tender. Add the milk, tomatoes, peas and lime juice. Heat through.

Chili

Ingredients:
2 lbs. ground beef
2 cloves garlic, chopped
1 (8oz) can tomato sauce
2 Tbsp chili powder
1 tsp ground cumin
1 tsp ground oregano
1 tsp salt
¼ tsp cayenne pepper
¼ cup masa harina
1 (15oz) can kidney beans, drained and rinsed
1 (15oz) can pinto beans, drained and rinsed
Chicken stock, as needed
Cheddar cheese
Green onions, chopped
Tortilla chips
Lime wedges

Brown the ground beef and add the garlic. Add the tomato sauce, chili powder, cumin, oregano, salt, and cayenne. Stir together well and cover. Reduce heat to low. Simmer for one hour, stirring occasionally. If the mixture becomes dry, add ½ cup chicken stock, as needed.

After an hour, place the masa harina in a small bowl. Add ½ cup chicken stock and stir together with a fork. Dump the mixture in to the chili. Stir together well. Add the beans and simmer for 10 minutes. Serve with shredded cheddar, chopped onions, tortilla chips, and lime wedges.

Chinese Style Vegetable Noodle Soup

Ingredients:
4 cups chicken stock
1 garlic clove, lightly crushed
1-inch peeled cube of fresh ginger root cut into fine matchsticks
2 Tbsp soy sauce
1 Tbsp Apple cider vinegar
3 oz fresh shiitake or button mushrooms, stalks removed and thinly sliced
2 Green onions, thinly sliced
1 ½ oz vermicelli or other fine noodles
6 oz Cabbage shredded
Several sprigs of cilantro for serving

Pour stick into saucepan. Add the ginger, garlic soy sauce and vinegar. Bring to a boil then cover. Reduce heat to very low and allow to simmer for 10 minutes. Remove the garlic clove and discard it.

Add the sliced onions and mushrooms and bring the soup back to a boil. Simmer for five minutes uncovered stirring occasionally. Add the noodles and shredded cabbage. Simmer for 3-4 minutes or until the noodles and vegetables are just tender. Stir in the cilantro leaves. Simmer for a final minute and then serve the soup hot.

Clam Chowder
From the old Holton Family Cookbook

RECIPE FOR: Clam Chowder

SOURCE: Dorothy L. Holton

PREPARATION TIME: _____ SERVINGS: 12-15

10-12 med-lrg Clams
(Chopped fine - Save Juice)   1/4 c. lemon Juice
1/4 lb. Salt Pork or bacon   2 Bay leaves
1 1/2 c. Chopped Onion   2 tsp. Sugar
1 c. Chopped Celery   1 T. Worcestershire
3/4 c. diced potatoes (cooked)   1 tsp Thyme
3/4 c. dice carrots   1 T. Oregano leaves
2 c. cream style Corn   Salt & Pepper to taste
1 qt. tomatoes - chopped   Hot sauce to taste
2 c. V-8 Juice   1 stick Margarine
2 c. chicken broth   (may omit if bacon is rich)

Fry salt pork & chop fine - set aside. In fat saute well drained clams. Saute onions & celery in margarine. Combine all ingredients except corn & lemon juice. Simmer 45-60 minutes. Add corn & lemon juice. Add water and/or clam juice if too thick. Stir to keep from burning on bottom.

Cranberry Sauce

Ingredients:
12 oz bag fresh cranberries
1 cup sugar
1 strip of orange or lemon zest
2 Tbsp water
Salt and pepper to taste

Empty bag of cranberries into a saucepan and transfer ½ cup to a small bowl. Add one cup of sugar, 1 strip of zest, and two tablespoons of water to the pan and cook over low heat, stirring occasionally until the sugar dissolves and the cranberries are soft (about 10 minutes). Increase the heat to medium and cook until the cranberries burst (about 12 minutes). Reduce the heat to low and stir in the reserved cranberries. Add salt and pepper to taste. Cool to room temperature before serving.

Fish Dip
Andrew's recipe

Ingredients:
½ lb. fish
1 jalapeno pepper
¼ cup mayonnaise (more as needed)
¼ cup sour cream (more as needed)
Old Bay, to taste
1 fresh lemon

Mix equal parts mayonnaise and sour cream. Smoke the fish and a jalapeno pepper. Once the fish and jalapeno pepper are done smoking, chop them up together. Add the mayonnaise and sour cream to the fish. Add old bay to taste. Squeeze in some fresh lemon.

Ginger Lentil Soup
From the Camaraderie Café

Ingredients:
4 cups lentils
1 small onion (diced)
3 carrots (diced)
1 Tbsp cumin
1 Tbsp curry
1-inch ginger root
6 cloves garlic
¼ cup melted butter
2 ¼ Tbsp salt
2 Tbsp sugar
¾ Tbsp pepper

Pour the lentils into a mid-sized pot. Fill pot with water. Bring to a boil. Decrease heat to a simmer and cook on high for 20 minutes or until the lentils are semi soft. Add chopped carrots and onions. Cook for 10 minutes. Add cumin and curry. Cook for 10 minutes. Melt butter and add ginger and garlic. Hand blend into a mixture and then add to soup. Add other ingredients to soup. Cook for five more minutes.

Gumbo

Ingredients:
4 oz vegetable oil
4 oz all-purpose flour
1 ½ lb. raw shrimp (31-50 count)
2 quarts water
1 cup diced onion
½ cup diced celery
½ cup diced green bell pepper
2 Tbsp minced garlic
½ cup peeled, seeded and chopped tomato
1 Tbsp kosher salt
½ tsp freshly ground black pepper
1 tsp fresh thyme, chopped
¼ tsp cayenne pepper
2 bay leaves
½ lb. andouille sausage cut into ¼ inch pieces and browned
1 Tbsp file powder
½ lb. fresh or frozen okra
2 cups of cooked rice

Make the shrimp stock: Peel and devein the shrimp. Put the shrimp in the refrigerator and keep the shells out in a big pot on the stove with the water. Add a little salt and a few aromatics to the water to create a shrimp stock. Simmer the stock for about an hour and a half.

Make the roux: Preheat oven to 350 degrees. Place the oil and flour into Dutch oven and whisk together to combine. Place in oven uncovered and bake for 1 ½ hours taking out about three times during the course of cooking to stir with a whisk.

Once the roux is complete, bring it out of the oven and place it on the stove top on medium heat. Add the onion, celery, bell pepper and garlic. Stir continuously for about five minutes.

Add the tomato, salt, pepper, thyme, cayenne, and bay leaves. Stir this together until combined and then add the strained shrimp stock. Bring to a boil and then decrease the heat to low. Simmer for about 30 minutes.

When you are ready to serve, brown the andouille sausage on the stove top in olive oil. Add the sausage to the gumbo. Cook the shrimp in the sausage oil for about three minutes and then add them to the gumbo. Sauté the okra on the stove top in olive oil, and season with salt and pepper.

Serve over white rice and garnish with the sautéed okra.

Jerk Marinade

Ingredients:
½ onion
4 scallions
2-3 Tbsp fresh or dried thyme
1 ½ Tbsp fresh ginger
8 garlic cloves
1 Tbsp cinnamon
1 Tbsp allspice
1 Tbsp white pepper
½ Tbsp nutmeg
2 Tbsp dark brown sugar
2 Tbsp honey
2 Tbsp soy sauce
1 Tbsp bouillon
1 scotch bonnet or other hot pepper

Place ingredients in the food processor and process until pulverized. Place the meat in the marinade and marinate at least 2 hours, preferably overnight.

*This is great on chicken or shrimp. Reserve some of the marinade, prior to marinading the meat, to use as a dipping sauce or make another batch.

Lentil Soup with lemon and dill

Ingredients:
1 Tbsp olive oil
1 tsp cumin seeds
1 32 oz container chicken stock
2 cups water
1 ½ cups green lentils, rinsed and drained
3 carrots chopped
2 cloves garlic, minced
1 bay leaf
3 Tbsp lemon juice
Plain yogurt
½ cup lightly packed dill sprigs, chopped
2 green onions, chopped
Salt and pepper

In a sauce pan, heat oil over medium high heat. Add cumin
seeds. Cook 30 seconds. Stir in stock, water, lentils, carrots,
garlic, bay leaf and ½ tsp salt. Boil, reduce heat, simmer 25
minutes. Remove bay leaf. Add lemon juice. Season with
pepper. Serve with yogurt, dill and green onions.

Minorcan Clam Chowder
A favorite from St. Augustine

Ingredients:
1 can, finely chopped clams
½ lb. salt pork, diced
2 cups of canned crushed tomatoes
1 bell pepper, cored and diced
1 Tbsp thyme
1 Tbsp marjoram
2 cloves garlic, crushed
2 onions, diced
2 medium potatoes, diced
2 Tbsp diced datil peppers
2-3 cups of chicken stock
Salt and pepper to taste

In a stock pot, sauté pork until it gives off fat and begins to brown. Add onions, garlic, and bell peppers and cook until they are browned. Add datil peppers, thyme, marjoram, tomato, and potatoes. Bring to a boil, then reduce heat and simmer for 20 minutes. Add the stock. Return to a quick boil. Reduce to simmer again, and add clams, cooking for 10 minutes or until the potatoes are tender.

Old Fashioned Chicken Soup with Noodles
Recipe from Colette Holton

Ingredients:
2 quarts water
6 chicken breasts (skin off)
2-3 Tbsp salt
2 Tbsp parsley
2 celery stalks, whole
2-3 celery stalks, sliced
½ onion
1 onion, sliced
1 carrot, whole
2-3 carrots, sliced

Fill a stock pot with water and place over medium high heat. To the pot add, the chicken breasts, salt, parsley, whole celery stalks, ½ onion, whole carrot. Bring to a boil and boil for about 15 minutes. Reduce heat to medium and simmer for about an hour. Check from time to time to be sure liquid has not boiled away. Add water if necessary.

Remove vegetables from the stock and discard. Remove chicken from stock and chop up to bite size pieces. Add to stock the sliced celery, sliced onion, and sliced carrots. Return to a boil for five minutes. Reduce heat and simmer for about 20 minutes.

At this point you may serve in bowls over prepared pasta of your choice. Garnish with fresh parsley or sprinkle dried parsley over the top.

Picadillo
From my days at the Camaraderie Café

Ingredients:
1 Tbsp Olive Oil
3 ½ cloves garlic, chopped
¾ onion, chopped
¾ cup green bell pepper, chopped
1 ½ lbs. ground beef
½ (5oz) jar green olives, pitted and halved
2 ½ oz capers, rinsed and drained
2 Tbsp white vinegar
½ tsp salt
½ tsp freshly ground black pepper
½ tsp ground cinnamon
½ tsp ground cloves
1 dried bay leaf
1/8 tsp hot sauce
3 cups canned tomatoes, half-drained

Directions:
In a large stock pot, heat olive oil over medium heat. Sauté garlic, onion and green pepper until onions are transparent. Transfer onion mixture to a bowl and set aside. In the same pot, brown the ground beef.

In a small sauce pan, combine the olives, capers, vinegar, salt, pepper, cinnamon, cloves, bay leaf and hot sauce. Let simmer over medium heat for 10 minutes.

Place olive mixture and the onion mixture into the pot with the ground beef. Add the half-drained tomatoes and cook for 1 hour over medium heat; stirring occasionally.

Potato Leek Soup

Part 1 Ingredients:
¼ cup butter
2 cups chopped leeks (white part only, about 2 leeks)
2 medium onions, chopped
8 cups chicken stock
Salt and pepper to taste

Melt butter in a large saucepan. Add leeks and onions. Sauté 5 minutes over medium heat. Stir in chicken stock, salt, and pepper. Bring to a boil and simmer another 5 minutes.

Part 2 Ingredients:
¼ cup butter
1/3 cup all-purpose flour
3 cups diced potatoes

Melt butter in a small saucepan over medium heat. Add flour and cook 2-3 minutes, being careful not to brown the flour. Add to soup mixture stirring constantly. Cook soup until it returns to a boil and thickens. Add potatoes; cook until tender (approximately 10 minutes).

Salad Dressing

Whisk together:
3 Tbsp Olive Oil
1 Tbsp white wine vinegar
Pinch of dried basil
2 pinches of salt
1 tsp. Spike
¼ tsp. garlic powder

Salsa

This recipe is best if blended in a Vitamix mixer.

Ingredients:
½ medium onion, peeled and halved (2.5 oz)
Pickled sliced jalapeños (45 g)
¼ cup cilantro (5 g)
1 tsp lemon juice
½ tsp salt
6 tomatoes from whole peeled tomato can

1. Place onion, jalapeno, cilantro, salt, lemon juice and three of the canned tomatoes into the mixer.
2. Blend for 20 seconds
3. Add remaining tomatoes
4. Blend for 10 seconds; do not overmix

Spaghetti Sauce
Recipe from Colette Holton

Ingredients:
1 lb. ground beef
2 stalks celery, diced
1 medium onion, diced
½ green bell pepper, diced
4 cloves garlic, crushed
1 can tomato sauce
1 can whole peeled tomatoes
1 can tomato paste
1 small can of mushrooms (drained)
1 ½ tsp dried basil
1 ½ tsp dried oregano
Salt and pepper to taste
1 tsp. sugar
1 tsp coconut oil

Brown the ground beef in a pan with coconut oil. Add the celery, onion, green bell pepper, and garlic. Simmer until the veggies are soft. Add the tomato sauce, whole peeled tomatoes, tomato paste and the drained mushrooms. Stir it together and add the basil, oregano, salt, pepper and sugar. Simmer for three hours.

Spicy Pumpkin Soup w/ Mexican Cream and Toasted Pepitas

Spicy Pumpkin Soup Ingredients:
3 Tbsp butter
3 cups finely chopped onions
1 (15oz) can of solid pack pumpkin
1 cup whole milk
¾ tsp dried crushed red pepper
2 ½ cups chicken broth
¾ cup shelled pumpkin seeds, toasted

Mexican Cream Ingredients:
¼ cup sour cream
¼ cup coconut milk
½ tsp fresh lime juice

Spicy Pumpkin Soup Directions:
In a large heavy metal pot, melt butter over medium heat. Add onions and sauté until translucent (about 10 minutes). Add to pot: Pumpkin, milk, and crushed red pepper and stir. Remove pot from stove and pour mixture into a food processor and puree. Return pureed mixture back to pot and add chicken broth. Simmer for 10 minutes to blend flavors, stirring occasionally. Season with salt and pepper to taste. Ladle soup into bowls, add a dollop of Mexican cream mixture and sprinkle with toasted pepitas.

Mexican Cream Directions:
In a small bowl, whisk sour cream, coconut milk and fresh lime juice. Cover and chill for 2 hours. Mexican cream can be made 1 week ahead, but keep chilled.

Serve the dish in bowls, a gourd, or in a small pumpkin. Top soup with the Mexican cream.

Taco Seasoning

Ingredients:
1 Tbsp dried onion flakes
1 tsp all-purpose flour
1 tsp beef bouillon
1 tsp garlic salt
1 tsp ground cumin
1 tsp paprika
1 tsp chili powder
¼ tsp cayenne pepper
¼ tsp white sugar

Combine all ingredients. Melt together with ¼ cup hot water.
Add to browned ground meat (beef, turkey, pork, etc.)

Tome Yum Goong

Ingredients:
4 cups chicken stock
3 stalks fresh lemongrass
12 fresh wild lime leaves
6 fresh chilis
1 lime, juiced (about 2 ½ Tbsp)
3 green onions
1 Tbsp roasted chili paste
1 cup canned straw mushrooms, drained
½ lb. peeled and deveined shrimp
2 Tbsp fish sauce

In a large saucepan, bring stock to boil over medium heat. Trim the lemongrass stalks. Cut away and discard the grassy tops leaving stalks about six inches long. Bruise each stalk on all sides. Add the bruised lemongrass and six of the lime leaves to the boiling stock and reduce heat to simmer. Cook until stock is fragrant and the lemongrass has turned a dull khaki green (about 5 minutes). Stem the chilies and place them under the flat side of a chef's knife. Crush them gently until they begin to split. Place the crushed chilis in a large serving bowl and add the lime juice, green onions and the remaining lime leaves. Set aside. Remove and discard the lemongrass. Turn on high and add the chili paste and mushrooms. Boil for 1 minutes. Add the fish sauce and shrimp. Cook until the shrimp are pink; about 1 minute. Remove soup from heat and quickly pour it into the serving bowl. Stir quickly to combine and season as desired.

White Sauce from Alabama
Andrew's BBQ sauce

Ingredients:
Black pepper – 2 tsp
Salt – 3 dashes or ½ tsp
Apple cider vinegar ¼ cup
Mayonnaise ½ cup
Horseradish 1 tsp
Hot sauce 3 dashes
Lemon juice 1 squeeze
Sugar 1 tsp

Whisk all ingredients together and store in a mason jar.

SIDES

Beer Bread

Ingredients:
3 cups self-rising flour
½ cup sugar
12 oz beer
2 Tbsp melted butter

Preheat oven to 375 degrees. Grease pan and set aside. In a large bowl, combine all ingredients. Mixture should be sticky. Pour into loaf pan. Bake for 45 minutes and then remove from the oven to brush with melted butter and return to the oven. Bake 10 more minutes.

Black Beans

Ingredients:
1 can black beans
2 cloves garlic, chopped
2 tsp olive oil
½ cup chicken stock
Salt and pepper

Drain and rinse beans. Heat up the oil and put in the garlic for a minute. Season with salt and pepper. Add the beans and chicken stock and cook on medium high for about five minutes.

Bread from the Isle of Lewis
A recipe from Heidi's travels to Scotland

Ingredients:
375 grams of flour
1 pack of instant yeast
1 tsp salt
3 Tbsp sugar
Olive oil, one splash
¾ cups warm water (or enough to make a dough)

Mix all together in a bowl and knead by hand for 10 minutes (I opt for the Kitchen aid mixer with the dough hand attachment). Cover and allow to rise for about 40 minutes. Knock out the air and knead again briefly into a tight ball. Place in an oiled loaf pan and allow to rise again. Bake for 35 minutes at 350 degrees.

Bread Recipe using a starter
Recipe from Woodeane from Upper Cut Salon

Feed the starter every 3-10 days. Keep the starter in the refrigerator in the meantime. To feed the starter, pull the jar out of the refrigerator and feed it:

3 Tbsp instant dried mashed potatoes
¾ cups white sugar
1 cup warm water

Leave the starter on the counter for 6-8 hours (or overnight). Once it has sat for that amount of time, mix up your bread:

Ingredients:
3 cups bread flour
1 tsp salt
3 Tbsp white sugar
1/8 cup olive oil
1 – 1 ½ cups of bread starter

Mix the dough with your hand until it comes together to form a ball. Place the ball in a bowl, cover it with a tea towel and allow it to rise for about 6 hours.

Punch it down after it has risen and then knead the dough on a floured surface about 25 times. Place in an oiled loaf pan and allow to rise (about 6 hours)

Bake at 350 degrees for about 45 minutes

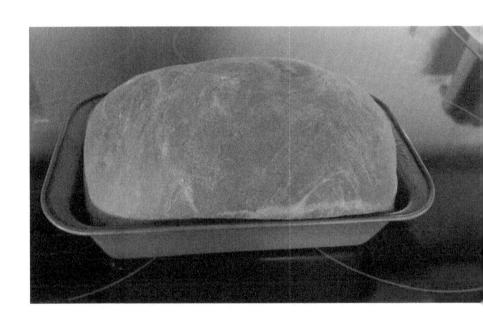

Collard Greens

Ingredients:
1 bunch collard greens
2 cloves garlic roughly chopped
Salt/pepper to taste
1 Tbsp olive oil
1 Tbsp chicken stock
1 Tbsp white wine vinegar

Preheat oven to 450 degrees. Rough chop the collard greens and combine in a bowl with garlic, salt, pepper, and olive oil. Put in a foil pouch and add 1 Tbsp chicken stock. Seal up and put I oven for 25 minutes. Remove, open pouch and add vinegar.

Dandelion Greens

Ingredients:
50 dandelion greens (approximately)
4 cups chicken stock
1 Tbsp butter
½ tsp lemon pepper seasoning

Remove greens from stem and discard the stem. Boil the greens in the chicken stock. Reduce heat to low and simmer for 10 minutes. Drain water. Add butter and lemon pepper and stir to combine.

Dinner Rolls

Recipe from my mother-in-law, Susan Tipler

Ingredients:
1 cup water
½ cup butter (1 stick)
½ cup shortening
¾ cup sugar
1 ½ tsp salt
1 cup warm water 105-115 degrees
2 packages of dry yeast
2 eggs, slightly beaten
6 cups all-purpose flour

Boil one cup water in a saucepan. Set off stove. Add butter and shortening and stir until melted. Add sugar and salt. Cool to lukewarm.

In a large bowl, put one cup warm water. Sprinkle yeast over top and stir to dissolve. Add butter/shortening mixture and eggs to dissolved yeast. Add six cups flour or enough to make a thick dough and mix thoroughly. Cover and put in refrigerator overnight.

About 2-2 ½ hours before serving rolls, turn dough out on floured board. Roll to desired thickness of about 1/3-1/4", cut and shape (cut with round biscuit cutter, brush with butter, fold in half, and place in greased pan). Pour more butter over folded rolls. Let rise about 1 ½ -2 hours. Bake at 400 degrees for 12-15 minutes or until well browned.

Eggplant Casserole
From the old Holton Family Cookbook

RECIPE FOR: Eggplant Casserole

SOURCE: Mom

PREPARATION TIME: _____ SERVINGS: _____

2 eggplant - Cut into cubes, boiled + drained.

2/3 C skim milk

1 egg

Saltines (Crushed) to cover bottom of Casserole dish.

Salt & Pepper to taste.

Grated Cheddar Cheese

Cover bottom of greased Casserole dish with crackers. Pour in eggplant. Beat egg, milk, & salt & Pepper - pour over eggplant. Cover with cheese. Bake @ 350° until set.

Mom made a version with oysters too.

Great Northern Beans

Ingredients:
1 bag of Great Northern Beans
3-4 cups Chicken Stock
1 onion, chopped
1 ham hock
1 tsp salt

Wash beans. Combine all ingredients in crock pot and cook on low for 12 hours.

Homemade Noodles

Ingredients:
3 egg yolks
1 whole egg
3 Tbsp cold water
1 tsp salt
2 cups flour

Beat egg yolks with whole egg until very light. Add water and salt; beat together. Stir in flour. Shape into four balls and then roll flat (the thinner the better). Cut noodles as desired.

Japanese Style Zucchini

Ingredients:
1 medium zucchini, halved and then sliced into 8ths lengthwise
½ medium onions, cut into chunks
½ tsp Sesame seeds
1 Tbsp olive oil
1 Tbsp soy sauce
½ lemon, juiced
Salt, to taste

Heat a flat pan or griddle until hot. Put olive oil on the griddle and add veggies. Move them around until they start to become soft. Add the sesame seeds. Add the soy sauce. Add a little salt. Squeeze the lemon using a knife to guide the stream.

Naan Bread

Ingredients:
1 cup warm water or bread starter
1 Tbsp sugar
2 tsp active dry yeast (if not using bread starter)
1 tsp salt
3 cups flour

Combine warm water (or bread starter), with sugar, and yeast (if not using bread starter). Let stand for five minutes or until foamy.

Add salt and flour. Mix thoroughly. Knead dough about 25 times and then form a tight ball. Put dough in an oiled bowl and cover with a damp towel for about 40 minutes.

Turn dough out onto floured board. Divide dough into 8 pieces and roll out with a rolling pin very thin.

Heat a cast iron pan to very hot and cook each piece 1-2 minutes per side. Don't worry if they look burnt (that's a good thing).

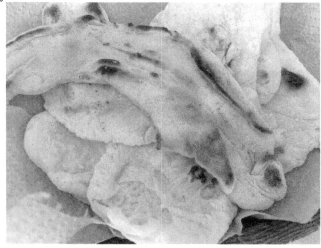

Plantains

Ingredients:
2-3 ripe (almost rotten) plantains
1-2 cups coconut oil (or enough to come up about ½ inch in a steep sided skillet
Brown sugar
Salt

Heat oil over medium high heat until hot. Meanwhile, slice the plantains into ½ inch thick circles. To cook the plantains, work in batches so that there is one layer of plantains on the bottom of the pan. When the oil is hot, place a batch of plantains in the oil. Cook until brown on one side and then flip over. Cook until brown on other side and flip over. Continue cooking until the plantains have a very dark brown color. Remove from oil and place on a wire rack. Place your next batch of plantains in the oil. While they are cooking, dust your first batch with salt and brown sugar. When the oil has dripped off of your first batch, remove to a serving plate. Continue this process until all plantains are finished.

Rice with Green Pepper & Mushrooms
From the old Holton Family Cookbook

RECIPE FOR: _____

SOURCE: _Mary Lee Dell_____

PREPARATION TIME: _____ SERVINGS: _____

Rice with green Pepper & Mushrooms

Green peppers	Celery
mushrooms	rice
chicken broth	onions
chicken	butter

Sautee- peppers, onions, and celery
        in butter until tender.

Cook- rice in broth.

Add- to the onions, pepper, & Celery,
        mushrooms and more broth.

Stir- entire mixture into rice.

Serve with baked chicken on top.

Scalloped Potatoes
From my mom, Colette Holton

Ingredients:
2 cups potatoes, thinly sliced
½ onion, thinly sliced
½ stick butter
Salt and pepper

Directions: Melt 2 Tbsp butter in nonstick skillet. Add onions and move around to coat with butter. Add potatoes and more butter and move around to coat. Add 3 pinches of salt and a grind of pepper. Stir and then allow to cook for a while over medium heat. Add more butter and turn. Continue doing this until golden brown. Lower the heat as the potatoes cook through.

Shishido Peppers

Ingredients:
2-3 cups of whole Shishido peppers
1 Tbsp Olive oil
Salt and pepper to taste
1 Tbsp Soy sauce

Directions: Rinse and drain Shishido peppers. Place them in a bowl with the olive oil and salt and pepper to taste. Toss them. Heat a skillet on medium high heat. Place the prepared peppers in the skillet and sauté until they begin to show signs of skin blistering. You don't want to overcook them, but they definitely need a little charring on their skin. Remove from heat and toss with the soy sauce.

Squash Casserole
From Aunt Jean Johnson in Florence, AL

Ingredients:
2 lbs. yellow squash, cooked and drained
1 onion, chopped
1 can cream of chicken soup
Salt and pepper to taste
1 (8oz) carton sour cream
1 package seasoned herb stuffing mix (preferably Pepperidge Farm brand)
1 stick butter
1 can water chestnuts, sliced (optional)

Melt butter and toss with stuffing mix. Set aside. Mix all other ingredients in a large bowl. Add half of stuffing. Mix. Pour into greased casserole and top with remaining stuffing mix. Bake at 350 degrees for 30-35 minutes. Freezes nicely. Fits a 13" Pyrex.

Stuffing

Ingredients:
2-4 cups turkey or chicken stock
3 stalks celery, diced
1 small onion, diced
1 loaf white bread, toasted and cubed
1 Tbsp butter
Salt and pepper, to taste
1 Tbsp dried parsley flakes

If you are making the stock, boil the turkey or chicken pieces with celery, carrot, onion, parsley and salt. Simmer stock for approximately 2 hours.

Sauté the diced celery and onion in butter, salt, and pepper until softened. In a big bowl, combine the toasted white bread and sautéed celery and onion. Add broth until moist. Add salt and pepper to taste. Add parsley. Grease pan and put mixture into the pan. Cook in a 350-degree oven for 45 minutes.

Sweet Cornbread

Ingredients:
½ cup cornmeal
1 ½ cups flour
2/3 cup sugar
1 Tbsp baking powder
½ tsp salt
1/3 cup oil
3 Tbsp melted butter
1 Tbsp honey
2 eggs, beaten
1 ¼ cups milk

Preheat oven to 350 degrees. Melt the butter. Combine the dry ingredients. Add the oil, melted butter, honey, eggs and milk. Pour into greased 8X8 pan. Bake for 35 minutes.

Tangy Ham Roll-ups
Recipe that I brought to the Grove Park Inn holiday party

Ingredients:
Cold cut ham, thinly sliced
8 oz. softened cream cheese
1 Tbsp fresh dill, chopped
1 jar pimento-stuffed olives

Mix dill with cream cheese. Spread on ham slices. Place olives in the center of each ham slice. Roll and chill for about 1 hour. Cut into 1-inch slices. Serve chilled.

Tracey's Crispy Pitas

Recipe from Tracey Munro when we evacuated from Key West because of Hurricane George and stayed at the Beach House in St. Augustine

Ingredients:
Pitas
Garlic Cloves
Olive Oil

Preheat oven to 400 degrees. Cut the pitas in half and pour olive oil on both sides and on the inside. Rub crushed garlic on both sides and on the inside. Bake at 400 degrees until the ends turn brown.

ENTREES

Asian Pork with Rice

Ingredients:
1 lb. ground pork
1 cup rice
2 cups water
2 cloves garlic, roughly chopped
2 stalks celery, sliced on an angle
10oz bok choy, snow peas, or broccoli, chopped
1 Tbsp soy sauce
2 Tbsp sherry vinegar
2 Tbsp black bean sauce
1 Tbsp sesame oil
1 tsp sesame seeds
Salt and pepper to taste
Olive oil as needed

Prepare the rice by boiling water with rice and simmering with a pinch of salt, covered, for 20 minutes. Combine your vegetable of choice and garlic in a bowl. Combine the black bean sauce, soy sauce, vinegar, and 2 Tbsp of water in a separate bowl.

Heat a drizzle of olive oil over medium high heat and add the pork. Cook without stirring for about three minutes. Season with salt and pepper and continue cooking until brown, breaking the meat apart with a spatula. Add the black bean sauce mixture and stir to coat the meat.

Meanwhile, heat sesame oil in a separate pan until hot. Add the celery. Cook, stirring occasionally for about three minutes. Add the vegetable/garlic mixture and continue cooking for a minute or so.

Combine the cooked vegetables with the meat. Serve over rice and garnish with sesame seeds.

Baked Chicken

Ingredients:
4-5 lb. chicken
2 cloves garlic
1 Tbsp chopped fresh basil
1 Tbsp chopped fresh oregano
1 Tbsp chopped fresh thyme
2-3 Tbsp olive oil
4 potatoes, peeled and quartered
4 carrots, peeled and cut into thirds
1 cup chicken stock

Preheat oven to 400 degrees. Pat chicken dry and place chicken in a large roasting pan or Dutch oven. Place garlic in chicken cavity and sprinkle with salt and pepper to taste. Mix olive oil, oregano, thyme, and basil. Spread the mixture over the chicken. Place potatoes and carrots around chicken. Add the broth. Cover and bake for two hours. Uncover and bake for an additional 15-20 minutes to brown chicken.

Bar-B-Que Chicken
Inspired by my dad, David Holton

Ingredients:
Whole chicken, cut into pieces
Worcestershire sauce
Olive Oil
Garlic Powder
Salt
Black Pepper

Combine the ingredients in a bowl and allow to marinate (overnight if possible). Start your grill and add the chicken once the grill is ready turning every so often until the internal temperature is 165 degrees.

Sauce: Whisk together the following ingredients
Ketchup
Worcestershire sauce
Salt
Pepper
Garlic powder

Beef Bourguignon

Ingredients:
2 slices of bacon
1 ½ lb. beef cubes
1 can Golden Mushroom soup
1 bay leaf
2 large cloves of garlic, minced
½ cup dry red wine or bouillon
2 Tbsp chopped parsley
1 ½ cups tiny white onions

In a large pan, cook bacon until crisp; remove. In drippings, brown beef. Add soup, wine, garlic, bay leaf, parsley and bacon. Cover; cook 1 hour or until tender. Remove bay leaf. Serve with buttered noodles.

Beef Stroganoff

Ingredients:
1 lb. strip steak, cut into thin strips
All-purpose flour, as needed
Seasoning salt, to taste
2 Tbsp olive oil
2 Tbsp butter
1 onion, sliced
8 oz mushrooms, sliced
1 (10oz) can beef broth
1 (10oz) can cream of mushroom soup
1 cup sour cream
Prepared egg noodles

Cut the steak and season with the seasoning salt. Dust with flour. Melt the butter and olive oil over medium high heat and brown the meat on all sides. Remove the steak from the pan.

Add the onions and mushrooms to the pan drippings. Sauté until tender. Sprinkle with 1 tsp of flour.

Add the steak back to the pan and combine with the onion and mushrooms. Add the cream of mushroom soup and beef broth. Cover and simmer over low heat for 30 minutes. Taste and add seasoning as desired. Stir in the sour cream right before serving.

Brent's Pasta

Ingredients:
1 package of homemade fettuccini
1 Tbsp nutritional yeast
1 (8oz container) Kalamata olives, chopped
1 (8oz container) fresh feta cheese in water, crumbled with water reserved
1 tsp Spike seasoning

Prepare noodles and set aside. Reserve some of the pasta water. Add olives, feta and yeast. Wet mixture with reserved pasta water and reserved feta water.

Cha-cha-cha casserole

Ingredients:
1 can (7 ounces) whole green chiles, drained
1 lb ground turkey or chicken
1 cup chopped onion
3 cloves garlic, minced
1 Tbsp chili powder or to taste
1 tsp salt
1 tsp ground cumin
1 can (about 14 oz) diced tomatoes with green chiles
2 cups frozen corn, thawed, or canned corn, drained
1 can (16 oz) refried beans
2 cups (8 oz) shredded Mexican cheese blend
2 cups crushed tortilla chips
1 cup diced tomato
½ cup sliced green onions

Preheat oven to 375 degrees. Spray 8-inch square baking dish with cooking spray. Cut chiles in half lengthwise; place in single layer in prepared dish.

Spray a medium nonstick skillet with cooking spray. Cook and stir meat, onion, garlic, chili powder, salt and cumin over medium heat until the meat is no longer pin. Add tomatoes with chiles; cook 10 minutes or until liquid evaporates.

Spoon meat mixture over chiles; top with corn and beans. Sprinkle with cheese and crushed chips. Bake 30 minutes. Let stand 5 minutes before serving. Garnish with fresh tomato and green onions.

Chicken Fricassee
Inspired by Coco's Cantina previously located on Cudjoe Key

Ingredients:
1 Tbsp coconut oil
½ cup coconut milk
½ cup chicken stock
1 onion, chopped
6 garlic cloves, chopped
½ green bell pepper, chopped
4 small whole peeled potatoes
3 carrots, peeled and cut into thirds
1 (8oz) can tomato sauce
½ cup dry white wine
½ Tbsp cumin
1 leaf fresh sage
Salt and pepper to taste
1 lb. boneless chicken thighs, cubed (you can really use one pound of any part of the chicken)

Put all items in a crock pot and cook on low for 6-8 hours.

Chicken Pot Pie

Ingredients for crust:
1 ¼ cups all-purpose flour
1 tsp sugar
¼ tsp fine salt
½ cup (1 stick) unsalted butter
3-5 Tbsp ice water

Ingredients for filling:
4 Tbsp butter
½ cup onion, diced
½ cup carrots, diced
½ cup celery, diced
½ cup green beans, cut
3 cups chicken, cooked and shredded
¼ cup flour
3 cups chicken stock
White wine, splash
¼ tsp turmeric
Salt and pepper to taste
1 tsp fresh thyme
1 tsp fresh parsley
¼ cup half and half

Preheat oven to 375 degrees.
Place the ingredients for the crust in a food processor and process until combined. Roll crust between two pieces of wax paper and then put the bottom crust in the pan.

On the stove top, melt butter over medium high heat. Sauté onion, carrots, celery, and green beans. Add the chicken, flour, broth, wine, turmeric, salt, pepper, thyme, parsley, and half and half. Stir together and then pour the mixture into the crust. Place the top crust on, brush with an egg and water mixture. Cut several slits in the top. Bake for 30 minutes or until desired color is achieved on the top.

Chicken Tandoori

Ingredients:
1 lb. of boneless, skinless chicken
1 lemon, juiced
Kosher salt
½ cup, plus 2 Tbsp plain yogurt, divided
1 Tbsp vegetable oil
½ small red onion, roughly chopped
3 garlic cloves, smashed
1 (2") thumb of ginger, peeled and chopped
4 tsp tomato paste
2 tsp ground coriander
1 ½ tsp ground cumin
1 ¾ tsp paprika
2 Tbsp fresh cilantro, chopped

Toss chicken with lemon juice and 1 ½ tsp salt. Pulse 2 Tbsp yogurt, vegetable oil, onion, garlic, ginger, tomato paste, coriander, cumin, 1 ½ tsp paprika, and ½ tsp salt in food processor. Toss chicken in mixture and let marinate for at least 15 minutes.

Preheat broiler. Place chicken on foil lined pan. Broil, turning once until slightly charred (approximately 8 minutes/side).

Combine the remaining ½ cup yogurt and ¼ tsp paprika, the cilantro, and a pinch of salt in a bowl. Top the chicken with the yogurt sauce and serve with Naan.
*you can toss sliced eggplant and orange bell peppers in with the chicken before cooking

Cuban Pork Roast

Ingredients:
1 boneless pork roast
1 grapefruit
1 lemon
1 lime
1 orange
2 Tbsp brown sugar
¼ cup white vinegar
1 ½ tsp salt
Black pepper to taste
3 Tbsp bacon fat
1 onion
½ tsp cumin
½ tsp oregano

In a crock pot, put bacon fat and allow to melt. Put the pork roast into the crock pot and season with salt and pepper. Squeeze citrus over meat. Add everything else and stir together. Cook 6-8 hours on low.

Curry Chicken Over Rice

Recipe from Chef Dawn Runge from the Little Palm Island Employee Kitchen

Ingredients:
1 lb. Boneless Chicken, cubed
1 can coconut milk
2 cups chicken stock
1 onion, large diced
1 red pepper, large diced
1 potato, large diced
2 carrots, large diced
2 celery, large diced
2 tsp curry powder (or to taste)
¼ cup white wine
1 Tbsp coconut oil
3 Tbsp cornstarch
Cayenne pepper to taste
Crushed red pepper to taste
Salt and pepper to taste

In a large pot on the stove top, heat coconut oil. Add the cubed chicken and cook through. Add the onion and red pepper. Cook for five minutes. Add other veggies, stock, coconut milk, spices and wine. Simmer for one hour. Melt cornstarch in a small amount of hot stock. Add to pot. Simmer until broth thickens.

Prepare your rice in a separate pot. You can substitute equal parts stock and coconut milk for the water to make the rice extra flavorful.

Serve the Curry Chicken in a bowl over the rice.

Enchiladas
Recipe from Cari Eggleston

Ingredients:
8-12 corn tortillas
¼ lb cooked protein (chicken, ground beef, turkey, etc.)
½ onion, diced
4 oz sliced black olives
8 oz shredded Mexican cheese
2 cans of red enchilada sauce
2 green onions, sliced

Pre-heat oven to 400 degrees. Coat the bottom of a 9X12 glass baking dish with ½ cup red enchilada sauce. Roll tortillas with a spoonful of red enchilada sauce, cooked protein, diced onion, black olives, and Mexican cheese. Place the rolled tortillas in the pan as you make them. Pour the remainder of the red enchilada sauce over the tortillas and top with the remainder of the Mexican cheese. Cover the dish with aluminum foil and back for 20 minutes or until the cheese is bubbly. Serve topped with green onions.

Fish Adobado

Recipe inspired by Chico's Cantina in Key West

Ingredients:
16 oz fish (mahi, cobia, or other sturdy fish)
5-6 ancho chilis (dried)
4 cloves garlic
1/3 cup apple cider vinegar
Vegetable oil as needed
1 Tbsp brown sugar
3-4 limes
1 red onion, sliced
1 bunch cilantro
Salt and pepper, to taste
2 cups water
Corn husks, package

Prepare marinade. Heat oil over medium heat. Put oil in pan and fry each piece of dried chili on each side for 10 seconds. Place chilis in two cups of hot water for 20 minutes.

In a food processor, blend chilis w/water, garlic, lots of salt, pepper, sugar, and vinegar until smooth. Cut up fish and marinate for up to overnight.

Soak corn husks in water before using to soften them. Take fish out of marinade and squeeze one lime over the entire batch of fish. Wrap each piece of fish in a corn husk. Grill until just done.

Serve with cilantro, salsa, and yellow rice.

Flavorful Roast Chicken

Ingredients:
4 tsp salt
2 tsp white sugar
¼ tsp ground cloves
¼ tsp ground allspice
¼ tsp ground nutmeg
¼ tsp ground cinnamon
1 whole chicken (about four pounds)
5 cloves of crushed garlic

Pat the chicken dry. In a bowl, mix the salt, sugar, cloves, allspice, nutmeg, and cinnamon. Rub chicken with the mixture inside and out. Cover the chicken and refrigerate it for 24 hours.

Pre-heat the oven to 500 degrees.

Stuff the chicken cavity with garlic. Place chicken, breast side down on a rack in the roasting pan.

Roast 15 minutes in preheated oven.

Reduce heat to 450 degrees and continue roasting for 15 minutes.

Baste chicken with pan drippings and then reduce heat to 425 degrees. Continue roasting for 30 minutes.

Let stand for 20 minutes before serving.

Fried Chicken

Ingredients:
1 chicken (3-4 pounds)
2 cups buttermilk
4 Tbsp salt
4 Tbsp Hungarian paprika
4 tsp garlic powder
1 ½ cups flour for dredging
Peanut oil for frying

Cut the chicken into 8 pieces. Place the pieces in buttermilk for up to 24 hours. In a small bowl, mix together the salt, paprika, and garlic powder. When you are ready to fry the chicken, drain the buttermilk and place the chicken on a sheet pan. Sprinkle all sides with the spice mixture. Dredge each piece in flour to coat. Heat up the peanut oil over medium heat until the oil is hot. Place chicken in the oil. Fry for 9 minutes on each of two sides. Place on a sheet pan covered with a wire rack.

Hot Wings
Inspired by my days working at Hooter's

Ingredients:
Chicken wings, cut into drumettes and flying parts
Salt & Pepper
Garlic powder
Paprika
½ stick butter
¼ cup Crystal hot sauce
Vegetable shortening

Preheat oven to 350 degrees. Place chicken wings on greased baking sheet. Sprinkle the wings on all sides with salt, pepper, garlic powder, and paprika. Bake for 30 minutes.

Meanwhile, melt the butter in a small sauce pan. Add crystal and ¼ tsp garlic powder. Whisk together.

When wings come out of the oven, toss them with ½ of the sauce and return to the pan. Return the pan to the oven and bake for an additional 10 minutes. Remove from the oven and toss with the remainder of the sauce.

Lasagna

Ingredients:
2 containers (15oz each) Ricotta cheese
2 cups shredded mozzarella cheese (about 8oz)
½ cup grated parmesan cheese
2 eggs
2 (10oz) can tomato sauce
1 (10oz) can diced tomatoes
12 uncooked lasagna noodles
Garlic powder, to taste
Italian seasoning, to taste
Salt and pepper, to taste
Olive oil, to taste

Preheat oven to 375 degrees.

In bowl, combine ricotta, 1 cup mozzarella, ¼ cup parmesan cheese, a generous sprinkle of garlic powder, and eggs.

To make the pasta sauce, in a separate bowl, combine tomato sauce, diced tomatoes, a splash of olive oil, a generous sprinkle of garlic powder, salt and pepper to taste, and a generous sprinkle of Italian seasoning.

In 13X9 inch baking dish, spread 1 cup pasta sauce. Layer 4 uncooked noodles, then 1 cup sauce and ½ of the ricotta mixture. Repeat. Top with remaining 4 uncooked noodles and 2 cups sauce. Cover tightly with aluminum foil and bake 1 hour.

Remove foil and sprinkle with remaining cheeses. Bake uncovered an additional 10 minutes. Let stand 10 minutes before serving. Serve with remaining sauce. Top with chopped fresh basil.

London Broil
Recipe from my mom, Colette Holton

Put the London Broil in a marinade of water, Worcestershire sauce, olive oil, salt, pepper, and garlic powder. Leave in marinade in the fridge for a few hours.

Make sure that the oven rack is close to the top burner. Turn the oven on Broil.

Place London Broil in a baking pan. Place in the oven for 5-6 minutes on one side. Flip it. Put in the oven for 5-6 minutes.

Don't get it too done or it will be tough. Cut to see if it is done to your preference.

Meatballs

Ingredients:
1 Tbsp bacon fat
1 lb. ground beef
½ tsp salt
1 small onion, diced
½ tsp garlic salt
1 ½ tsp Italian seasoning
¾ tsp dried oregano
¾ tsp crushed red pepper flakes
1 dash hot sauce
1 ½ Tbsp Worcestershire sauce
1/3 cup milk
¼ cup grated parmesan cheese
½ cup seasoned bread crumbs

Preheat oven to 400 degrees. Mix all ingredients together except the bacon fat and form into 1 ½" meatballs. Place on a baking sheet and bake for 15 minutes. Heat bacon fat in skillet. Toss meatballs in skillet until browned on outside.

Mississippi Mud Roast
Recipe inspired by Eric Peper

Ingredients:
1 Chuck roast (3-4 pounds)
1 stick of butter (1/2 cup)
1 packet of dried original ranch dressing mix
1 packet of dried Lipton onion soup
8-10 jarred whole pepperoncini peppers

Place the roast in the bottom of your crock pot. Place the stick of butter on top, right out of the refrigerator. Pour the dried ranch dressing and the dried onion soup over the top of the roast and butter. Place the pepperoncini peppers around the roast. Cook on low in the crock pot for 6-8 hours.

Pad Thai

Ingredients:
8 oz Thai noodles
2 Tbsp peanut oil
2 garlic cloves, minced
1 serrano chili, minced
2 cups bean sprouts
½ cup salted peanuts, chopped
½ cup cilantro, chopped
¼ cup brown sugar
¼ cup soy sauce
2 Tbsp rice vinegar
1 Tbsp lime juice
1 Tbsp fish sauce
1 lb. chicken breast, cut into bite sized pieces (raw)
2 more Tbsp soy sauce
2 Tbsp cornstarch
2 green onions, sliced

Marinate chicken breast pieces in a mixture of 2 Tbsp soy sauce and 2 Tbsp cornstarch. Set aside in the refrigerator.

Make the sauce by combining: brown sugar, ¼ cup soy sauce, rice vinegar, lime juice and fish sauce. Set aside.

Prepare noodles by soaking in hot water for 10 minutes. Drain and set aside.

Heat oil until hot and add garlic and serrano chili. Cook until fragrant and then add chicken. Cook until done.

Pour in the prepared sauce. Stir to combine.

Add noodles and toss to coat. Add green onions, cilantro, bean sprouts, and peanuts. Serve with additional lime slices.

Pizza Dough
A recipe from Heidi's trip to Italy

Ingredients:
1 envelope instant yeast
1 ½ cups warm water
½ tsp sugar
4 cups all-purpose flour
1 tsp salt

Add yeast, ½ cup flour, and the sugar to the warm water. Stir, let stand until foamy. Mix the remaining flour and salt in a bowl. Pour it into the yeast mixture. Knead into dough ball until elastic and smooth (I use the Kitchen aid mixer). Oil a large bowl, place the dough ball into it. Cover with a towel until it doubles in size. Remove dough, punch down and divide it into four parts. Shape into balls. Cover them with the kitchen towel and let them rise again. Once the rise, they are ready to use or store in plastic wrap in the refrigerator.

Quiche
From the Camaraderie Cafe

Ingredients:
32 oz half and half
5 eggs
Salt to taste
Tabasco sauce to taste
2 pie crusts
Filling of choice (spinach bacon and tomato, crab and swiss, use your imagination)

Preheat oven to 400 degrees. Par bake the two pie crusts for 5-10 minutes (poke small holes in the bottom before baking). Lightly beat the eggs and half and half together. Add the salt and tabasco sauce to the mixture. In the pre-baked pie shells, add in light layers of your selected ingredients. Pour the half and half mixture over the ingredients into the pie shells. Bake for 45 minutes.

Recipe for crust
Ingredients:
1 cup flour
½ tsp salt
¼ cup oil
¼ cup ice water

Mix flour and salt with fork. Beat oil and water with whisk to thicken. Pour into flour and mix with fork. Press into 9" pie crust. Fill with quiche and bake as suggested above.

Short Ribs

Ingredients:
5 lb. bone in short ribs cut into 2" pieces
Salt and pepper, to taste
3 Tbsp bacon fat
3 medium onions, chopped
3 carrots, peeled and chopped
2 celery stalks, chopped
3 Tbsp all-purpose flour
1 Tbsp tomato paste
1 750ml bottle of dry red wine
10 sprigs flat leaf parsley
8 sprigs thyme
4 sprigs oregano
2 sprigs rosemary
2 bay leaves
1 head garlic, halved crosswise
4 cups beef stock

Preheat oven to 350 degrees. Brown short ribs on all sides in bacon fat and transfer to a plate. In the drippings, sauté the onions, carrots, and celery over medium high heat. Add flour and tomato paste -3 minutes. Add wine, then short ribs. Bring to a boil and then lower heat. Simmer until wine is reduced by half (about 25 minutes). Add all herbs and garlic and stir in the stock. Bring to a boil, cover and transfer to oven. Cook for 2-2 ½ hours.

Shrimp Etouffee

Recipe from my sister, Heidi, from her interesting history in New Orleans

Ingredients:
1 stick of butter
¾ cup flour
1 onion, chopped
1 bell pepper, chopped
3 celery stalks, chopped
5-6 garlic cloves, chopped
1 cup of tomatoes, chopped
1 bunch of green onions, chopped (save a little for garnish)
2-3 cups chicken stock
2-3 bay leaves
Pinch of thyme
1-2 tsp of Cajun/creole seasoning (like Tony Chachere)
Salt and pepper
1 lb. shrimp (or you can substitute crawfish tails or chicken thighs)

Melt butter in a cast iron pot and stir in flour to make a rue (you are looking for a peanut butter color when it is ready). This will take 30-45 minutes, so plan ahead – make sure you've gone to the bathroom and have wine and your phone nearby, because you can't leave the stove. Sometimes you need to add more butter or flour. It should be thick enough for you to draw a heart in it.

Add onions and stir for 3-5 minutes.

Add celery, bell peppers, and garlic and stir another 5-10 minutes.

Add tomatoes, thyme, creole seasoning, salt and pepper and stir to combine.

Add 2 cups of chicken stock, a little at a time until it's the right consistency. You might need more than 2 cups.

Add bay leaves and bring to a quick boil.

Turn the heat down and simmer for 10 minutes. Add green onions and simmer another 10 minutes. Taste it and add more seasoning, if necessary. Add shrimp or your choice of seafood/chicken and cook until they're done. If using chicken, you will want to precook.

Serve with rice and remaining green onions.

Tomato Parsley Pasta

Ingredients:
4 handfuls of dried egg noodles
1 cup of Basic White Sauce (see recipe under soups/sauces)
2 chicken bouillon cubes
½ tomato, diced
Parsley flakes, to taste

Boil 4 cups of water with 2 bouillon cubes. Add the egg noodles once boiling and cook to desired texture; typically, 7-8 minutes. Drain pasta. Prepare Basic White Sauce recipe. Salt the tomatoes and set aside. Combine the noodles with the white sauce. Top with the salted tomatoes and the parsley flakes.

SALADS

Chinese Bitter Melon Salad

Ingredients:
1-2 Bitter Melon
Pot of water
Salt

Ingredients for dressing:
1 Tbsp olive oil
1 clove garlic minced
1 Tbsp ginger, minced
½ tsp sugar
2 Tbsp apple cider vinegar
2 Tbsp soy sauce
1 tsp sesame oil

Wash and slice bitter melons. Remove the seeds and rind. Springle with salt and marinate for 10 minutes. Blanch them in boiling water for 1 minute and then rinse. Allow melon to cool to room temperature.

Prepare the dressing by heating oil and then adding garlic and ginger. Remove from heat and stir in the remaining ingredients. Toss melon in the dressing and serve.

Chinese Noodle Salad
Recipe from Darinda Davis

Ingredients:
1 package Ramen Noodles, crushed (set the seasoning pack aside)
½ head cabbage or slaw mix chopped
4 scallions, sliced
½ cup slivered almonds, toasted
2 Tbsp sesame seeds, toasted
1/3 cup sesame oil
3 Tbsp red wine vinegar
2 Tbsp sugar
Salt and pepper to taste

Mix cabbage, scallions, almonds, sesame seeds, ad crushed soup noodles in a bowl. Mix soup seasoning packet with vinegar, oil, sugar, salt and pepper. Pour the dressing over the salad and toss. Best if refrigerated for an hour or so.

Curry Chicken Salad
Recipe from Riviera Palm Springs

Ingredients:
2 chicken breasts
2 cups mayonnaise
1 Tbsp + 1 tsp curry powder
¾ cup diced celery
¾ cup jalapeno, diced
¼ cup chopped red onion
½ Tbsp + ½ tsp chopped garlic
½ cup + 1 Tbsp lime juice
½ bunch chopped cilantro
Red or green grapes halved
Toasted cashews (6 minutes at 350 degrees)
Romaine hearts
Large tortillas

Mix curry powder and mayonnaise together.

Roast chicken with salt and pepper for 18 minutes at 350 degrees, let cool and dice.

Mix in large bowl chicken, mayo, celery, onion, lime juice, cilantro, garlic, jalapeno. Add salt and pepper to taste.

Mix romaine hearts, grapes, cashews to salad and serve with tortillas.

Green Papaya Salad

**Because we had so many papayas in the yard after
Hurricane Irma**

Ingredients:
2 cloves of garlic
¼ tsp salt
1 Tbsp dry-roasted salted peanuts
½ tsp sugar
2 Tbsp fresh lime juice
1 Tbsp fish sauce
2 Roma tomatoes
1 green papaya, seeded, peeled and shredded

In a mortar and pestle, combine the garlic, salt, peanuts and
sugar. Transfer to a large bowl and mix in the lime juice and
fish sauce. Add the tomatoes to the bowl. Add the seeded,
peeled and shredded papaya. Lightly toss together.

Kale Salad

Ingredients for salad:
1 bunch of Kale, stem removed and chopped
¼ cup cabbage, chopped
2/3 cup dried sour cherries or dried cranberries
1/3 cup nuts (whatever you have on hand)

Ingredients for dressing:
¼ cup olive oil
2 Tbsp maple syrup
2 Tbsp apple cider vinegar
1 tsp Dijon mustard
1 tsp zest from one lemon
½ lemon, squeezed
Salt and pepper to taste

Toast the nuts on the stovetop for about five minutes, moving constantly.

Place all dressing ingredients except for olive oil in a bowl. Slowly whisk in olive oil until it incorporates.

In a large bowl, add kale and cabbage. Mix in the cherries and nuts. Toss with the dressing.

Persimmon Salad

Ingredients:
4 ripe persimmons
2 Tbsp olive oil
2 Tbsp balsamic vinegar
4 Tbsp pomegranate seeds
4 tsp sour cream
4 tsp hazelnuts (or whatever nut you have)
Finishing salt to taste

Mix olive oil and balsamic vinegar together. Slice and toss persimmons in the mixture. Plate and arrange other ingredients with dollop of sour cream on each plate. Finish with salt.

St. Augustine Salad
Inspired by the Columbia Restaurant in St. Augustine, FL

Ingredients:
4 cups iceberg lettuce, broken into 1 ½" pieces
1 ripe tomato, cut into eighths
½ cup baked ham, julienned
½ cup Swiss cheese, julienned
½ cup pimiento-stuffed green Spanish olives
2 cups "1905" Dressing (see recipe that follows)
¼ cup Romano Cheese, grated
2 tablespoons Lea & Perrins Worcestershire Sauce
1 lemon

Combine lettuce, tomato, ham, Swiss cheese, and olives in a large salad bowl. Before serving, add "1905" Dressing, Romano cheese, Worcestershire, and the juice of 1 lemon. Toss well and serve immediately. Makes 2 full salads or 4 side salads.

"1905" Dressing
½ cup extra-virgin Spanish olive oil
4 garlic cloves minced
2 teaspoons dried oregano
1/8 cup white wine vinegar
Salt and pepper to taste

Mix olive oil, garlic, and oregano in a bowl. Stir in vinegar and season with salt and pepper. For best results, prepare 1 to 2 days in advance and refrigerate.

DESSERTS

Apple Dump Cake
Annabel's recipe from 1st grade

Ingredients:
42 oz apple pie filling (2 cans)
1 spice cake mix
½ cup butter, melted

Pour both cans of apple pie filling into a greased crock pot.
Combine dry cake mix and butter until crumbly. Sprinkle over
apple pie filling. Cook on low for four hours or on high for
two hours.

Anna's Chocolate Cake

Recipe from Anna Agnew from the Camaraderie Café

Ingredients:
1 box "moist" yellow cake mix
3 eggs
1/3 cup oil
¾ cup water
8 oz sour cream
¾ package semi-sweet chocolate chips
1 package of chocolate pudding

Preheat oven to 350 degrees. Mix all ingredients together and bake in a greased and floured bunt pan for 45 minutes to 1 hour.

Aunt Trudy's Sour Cream Pound Cake
Recipe from Rachel Ward

Ingredients:
1 cup butter
3 cups sugar, divided
3 cups flour
½ tsp salt
¼ tsp baking soda
6 eggs, separated
1 cup sour cream
1 tsp vanilla
1 tsp lemon extract

Cream butter with 2 cups sugar. Sift dry ingredients. Add egg yolks one at a time to butter mixture, mixing well after each addition. Alternately add dry ingredients and sour cream, beginning and ending with flour. Add vanilla and lemon extract. Beat egg whites until they form peaks. Add 1 cup sugar to the egg whites and beat until stiff. Fold into batter. Bake in a tube or Bundt pan at 350 degrees for approximately 1 hour. Test with a toothpick for doneness.

Blueberry Muffins
Recipe from my Grammy who used to work at Jordan Marsh (a department store)

½ cup butter (softened)
1 cup sugar
2 eggs
½ cup milk (less milk if using frozen berries)
2 ½ cups blueberries (save ½ cup to crush)

Sift together:
2 cups all-purpose flour
2 tsp baking powder
½ tsp salt

Grease 15 cup muffin pan. Preheat oven to 375 degrees. In a large bowl, with mixer at medium speed, cream butter and sugar until light and fluffy. Add eggs one at a time, beating well after each addition. To the creamed mixture, alternate adding the sifted ingredients and the vanilla and milk. Crush ½ cup of the berries. (do not mash) and add to the batter with the mixer. Fold in the remaining berries. Spoon into the muffin pan so that each cup is filled about ¾ full. Bake 30 minutes. Check at 25 minutes.

Bread Pudding
From the old Holton Family Cookbook

RECIPE FOR: _____

SOURCE: *Grandmama Lanier*

PREPARATION TIME: _____ SERVINGS: _____

Bread Pudding

2-3 cps. crumbled bread

½ cp sugar

1-2 eggs

milk to moisten

½-1 tsp lemon or nutmeg

Mix all ingredients together. (Let
soak if bread is very dry) Bake at
450° for 30 min.

Sauce

Boil 1 cp water, mix 1½ T flour in a
½ cp sugar. Add to boiling water.
Boil one or two minutes. Add flavor
(Lemon) and butter.
(Add food coloring for fun)

Cheesecake

Ingredients for sponge cake crust:
Unsalted butter, softened
1/3 cup sifted cake flour
¾ tsp baking powder
Pinch of salt
2 large eggs, separated
1/3 cup sugar
1 tsp vanilla extract
2 drops lemon extract
2 Tbsp unsalted butter, melted
¼ tsp cream of tartar

Ingredients for Cheesecake filling:
4 (8oz) packages of full fat cream cheese
1 2/3 cups sugar
¼ cup cornstarch
1 Tbsp vanilla extract
2 large eggs
¾ cup heavy cream

This must be made a day before you plan to enjoy it.

Start by making the crust. Preheat the oven to 350 degrees. Generously butter the entire inside of a 9-inch springform pan. Wrap the outside with aluminum foil.

Sift the flour baking powder and salt together in a small bowl.

In a large bowl, beat the egg yolks on high for three minutes. With the mixer running, add 2 Tbsp sugar and continue mixing until thick light yellow ribbons form in the bowl (about five more minutes). Beat in the vanilla and lemon extracts.

Sift the flour mixture over the batter and stir it in by hand until there are no remaining white flecks. Blend in the melted butter.

In another clean bowl, using clean, dry beaters, beat the egg whites and cream of tartar together on high until frothy. Gradually add the remaining sugar and continue beating until stiff peaks form (the whites with stand up and look glossy, not dry). Fold about one-third of the whites into the batter, then the remaining whites.

Gently spread the batter over the bottom of the prepared pan and bake for 10 minutes. Leave the crust in the pan and place on a wire rack to cool.

Leave the oven on while you prepare the batter for the cheesecake. Prepare a water bath.

In a large bowl, beat one package of cream cheese, 1/3 cup sugar, and the cornstarch together on low until creamy (about 3 minutes). Scrape down the bowl several times. Blend in the remaining cream cheese, one package at a time, beating well and scraping down the bowl after each addition.

Increase the mixer speed to medium and beat in the remaining sugar, then the vanilla. Blend in the eggs one at a time, beating well after each addition. Beat in the cream just until completely blended. Be careful not to overmix! Spoon the batter over the crust.

Place the cake in the water bath and then into the oven. Bake until the edge is light golden brown (approximately 1 ¼ hours). Remove the cheesecake from the oven and water bath. Transfer to a wire rack and let cook for 2 hours. Leave the cake in the pan covering loosely with plastic wrap and refrigerate overnight.

Cheesecake
From the old Holton Family Cookbook

RECIPE FOR: CHEESE CAKE

SOURCE: Dorothy Holton

PREPARATION TIME: _____ SERVINGS: _____

3- 8oz. pks. cream cheese(softened)

1¼ cp. sugar

1 pnt. sour cream

2 tsp vanilla

1 T finely grated lemon rind

6 egg yolks

3 T all purpose flour

1 T lemon juice

6 egg whites

Preheat oven- 350°. Cream softened
cheese by beating it with a spoon
until smooth. Gradually beat in
sugar, then egg yolks one at a time,
until well mixed. Stir in sour cream
flour, vanilla, lemon juice and rind.
Beat egg whites until stiff, fold in
to mixture until no streaks of white
show. Pour into cake shell and bake
for 1 hour. let cool for 15 minutes.

Cheese Cake Shell (Crust)
1 6oz Box Graham crackers Crushed (3/4 C)
2 T Sugar   1/2 tsp. Cinnamon
6 T Unsalted butter 2 T soft butter
Combine dry ingredients + stir in melted
unsalted butter. Heavily butter 9 x 3"
deep spring pan
Put even layer of crust on bottom + sides
Refridgerate.

Chocolate Avocado Pudding

Ingredients:
1 avocado, peeled, pitted, and cubed
¼ cup unsweetened cocoa powder
¼ cup brown sugar
3 Tbsp coconut milk
1 tsp vanilla extract
1 pinch cinnamon

Put all ingredients into food processor and blend until smooth.
Refrigerate until chilled (about 30 minutes)

Chocolate Chip Cookies

Ingredients:
2 sticks of butter
¾ cup granulated sugar
¾ cup packed brown sugar
1 tsp vanilla extract
2 eggs
2 ¼ cups all-purpose flour
1 tsp baking soda
½ tsp salt
2 cups milk chocolate chips

Heat the oven to 375 degrees. In a large bowl, combine butter, sugars, and vanilla until creamy. Add eggs. Mix well. Stir together combine dry ingredients. Gradually add dry ingredients to butter mixture. Stir in chocolate chips. Drop by teaspoons onto ungreased cookie sheet. Bake 8-10 minutes or until lightly browned.

Chocolate Icing

Ingredients:
1 cup butter, softened
½ cup cocoa powder, sifted
5 cups powdered sugar
1 tsp vanilla extract
3-4 Tbsp milk

Whip butter and cocoa until smooth. Stir in vanilla and powdered sugar. Slowly stir in milk.

Cream Cheese Icing

Ingredients:
1 8oz pack cream cheese
1 box confectioners' sugar
1 stick butter
1 tsp vanilla

Soften cream cheese and butter. Mix well with sugar and vanilla.
*you can add food coloring to this recipe

Crème Brulée

Ingredients:
2 cups heavy cream or half and half
1 vanilla bean, split lengthwise
1/8 tsp salt
5 egg yolks
½ cup sugar, plus more for the topping

Heat oven to 325 degrees. In a saucepan, combine cream, vanilla bean and salt. Cook over low heat until just hot. Let sit for a few minutes. Use a butter knife or spoon to scrape out the inside of the vanilla bean. Whisk the extraction into the cream while discarding the bean pod.

Set a pot of water on the stove to boil (this will be used for your water bath)

In a bowl, beat egg yolks and sugar together until light (I prefer to use the KitchenAid mixer). Stir about a quarter of the cream into this mixture, then pour sugar/egg mixture into the cream and stir.

Pour into 6oz ramekins and place ramekins in a baking dish. Fill baking dish with boiling water halfway up the sides of the ramekins. Bake for 30 to 40 minutes or until centers are barely set. Cool completely. Refrigerate for several hours and up to a couple of days.

When ready to serve, top each custard with about a teaspoon of sugar in a thin layer. Place ramekins under a broiler 2-3 inches from the heat source. Turn on the broiler. Cook until sugar melts and browns or even blackens a bit (about five minutes). Serve within two hours.

Dee's Donuts

Recipe from my dad, David Holton. It was a great family evening when he would make these for us as kids.

Ingredients:
1 can of refrigerated biscuits (like Grands or Pilsbury)
1 pot filled with about 1-2 inches of vegetable oil
Sugar to taste
Cinnamon to taste

Heat oil over medium high heat until hot. Meanwhile, open the can of biscuits and shape your donuts. You can shape them into small round balls or in the classic donut shape with a hole in the middle. When the oil is hot enough, put in a few of your donuts, but don't overcrowd them. Cook until they are slightly brown. Turn over and cook until they look golden. Remove them from the oil and place on a wire rack. Dust them with sugar and cinnamon to taste.

Gingerbread Cake
Recipe from my mom, Colette Holton

Sift together:
1 ¼ cup flour
1 tsp ground ginger
1 tsp baking soda
1 pinch salt

In a pot, heat together:
½ cup sugar
1/3 cup butter
1/3 cup molasses
1/3 cup light corn syrup

Heat oven to 325 degrees. Cool heated ingredients for five minutes. Add melted ingredients to dry ingredients. Rinse the pot that held the heated ingredients with ½ cup milk. Add the milk to the mixture as well as 1 beaten egg. Pour mixture into a greased and floured pan. Bake between 45 minutes to 1 hour. Cool. Ice with white icing or cream cheese icing.

Gingerbread Cookies
Recipe from Colette Holton

Ingredients:
½ cup butter
½ cup sugar
½ cup molasses
1 egg
3 cups all-purpose flour
1 Tbsp ground ginger
1 ½ tsp baking soda
1 tsp ground cinnamon
½ tsp salt
¼ tsp fresh ground pepper

Beat the butter, sugar, molasses and egg until fluffy. Combine flour, ginger, baking soda, cinnamon, salt and pepper. Gradually beat the flour mixture into the butter mixture until well blended. Wrap dough in plastic wrap and refrigerate for 2 hours.

Preheat oven to 350 degrees. Work with ¼ of the dough at a time. Cut into shapes after rolling out ½" thick on a floured surface. Place on ungreased cookie sheet. Decorate if desired. Bake for 8-15 minutes (or until golden brown).

Gingersnaps

A very special family recipe from Susan Tipler, my mother-in-law who is excellent at baking

Ingredients:
¾ cup shortening
1 cup brown sugar (packed)
1 egg
¼ cup molasses
2 ¼ cups all-purpose flour
2 tsp baking soda
1 tsp cinnamon
1 tsp ginger
½ tsp cloves
¼ tsp salt
Dish of granulated sugar

Mix thoroughly shortening, brown sugar, egg, and molasses. Blend in remaining ingredients except the dish of granulated sugar. Cover; chill for 1 hour.

Heat oven to 375 degrees. Shape dough by rounded teaspoonfuls into balls. Smaller balls are better, so maybe slightly less than a tsp each. Dip the balls into the dish of granulated sugar. Place balls 3 inches apart on a lightly greased baking sheet and gently press down on them to take them from ball to cookie shape. Bake 10-12 minutes or just until set (the top will have crackle lines on it). Immediately remove from baking sheet.

Grammy's Frozen Mold

My Grammy's holiday recipe to serve with holiday dinner

Ingredients:
1 cup dream whip (set aside)
3 oz. cream cheese (mix with 2 Tbsp. sugar, plus 2 Tbsp.
Mayonnaise)
1 cup whole cranberries (canned)
10 maraschino cherries (sliced)
1 4oz. can crushed pineapple
¼ cup chopped walnuts or pecans

Add fruit sauce to cheese.
Fold into dream whip.
Add nuts – mix well.
Pour into a mold.
Freeze several hours.
I typically double the recipe.

Hay Stacks

Ingredients:
2 cups peanut butter chips
2 cups butterscotch chips
2 cups chocolate chips
1 ½ cups crushed ripple potato chips
1 ½ cups peanuts

Mix together the peanut butter, butterscotch and chocolate chips in the top of a double broiler. Chop the peanuts in a food processor and crush the chips. Add the peanuts and potato chips to the melted mixture. Spoon into mini cupcake papers. Refrigerate until set.

Ice Cream

Ingredients:
2 cups heavy cream
1 cup half and half
2/3 cups sugar
6 egg yolks
*whatever flavoring you want to use)

Prepare ice water bath. Combine cream, half and half and sugar in a sauce pan and heat on medium heat until hot. (If making mint or vanilla, add the leaf or the pot to the sauce pan while heating)

Whisk egg yolks. Whisk a cup of the hot milk with the eggs and turn the heat to low. Add the eggs to the milks. Stir until it makes a custard. Strain through mesh strainer. Put in ice water bath. Put in refrigerator until very cool. Turn in ice cream maker. (If making mint chocolate chip, this is where you would add the chips)

Iron Skillet Apple Pie

Ingredients:
4 apples, peeled and sliced
1 tsp cinnamon
¾ cup white sugar
½ cup butter
1 cup brown sugar
2 Tbsp white sugar, for crust
2 pie crusts (one for top and one for bottom)

Use 10" cast iron skillet. Preheat oven to 350 degrees. Toss apples with 1 tsp cinnamon and ¾ cups white sugar. Set aside. Melt butter in skillet over medium heat. Add brown sugar and stir constantly for 2 minutes. Gently place bottom crust into skillet. Spoon apple mixture on top of crust. Add top crust. Sprinkle with 2 Tbsp white sugar. Cut five slits in the top. Bake in oven for 1 hour.

Key Lime Pie

Ingredients for graham cracker crust:
1/3 of a 1 lb. box of graham crackers
5 Tbsp unsalted butter, melted
1/3 cup sugar

Ingredients for filling:
3 egg yolks
2 tsp lime zest
1 (14oz) can sweetened condensed milk
2/3 cup key lime juice

Preheat oven to 350 degrees. Prepare the crust by putting the items in a food processor and process until combined. Press the mixture into a pie pan. Par-bake the crust for eight minutes.
Allow the crust to cool while you prepare the filling.

Beat egg yolks and zest for five minutes. Add sweetened condensed milk and mix for four minutes. Add key lime juice until just combined. Pour into cooked pie crust and bake for 10 minutes.

Key Lime Pie
From the old Holton Family Cookbook

RECIPE FOR: Key Lime Pie
SOURCE: Nila Vae Recipe?
PREPARATION TIME: _____ SERVINGS: _____

1 can Eagle brand Milk
1/2 c. lime juice
1 tsp. lime Rind
4 oz. Cream Cheese
1 egg yolk
1 egg white   Sugar
1/4 tsp. ~~baking powder (or soda)~~
Graham Cracker Crust

Cream the cream cheese. Add egg yolk
& beat until smooth. Add Milk, lime juice,
& Rind
In separate bowl beat egg white & ~~baking~~ sugar
~~powder (soda)~~ until white peaks.
Fold into other mixture. Pour into
pie shell. Chill. Serve with Cool Whip.

Lemon Cream Cheese Cookies

Recipe from my mom, Colette Holton

Ingredients:
¾ cup softened butter
3oz cream cheese
¾ cup granulated sugar
2 cups flour
¼ tsp salt
1 Tbsp Lemon juice
1 Tbsp lemon peel

Beat the butter, cream cheese, sugar and lemon together in one bowl. Mix the flour and salt together in another bowl. Combine the two mixtures and put the combination into ball form and refrigerate for 1 hour.

Preheat oven to 350 degrees. Flour surface and roll out dough into ¼ to ½ inch thick.

Cut out forms and put on pan.

Bake at 350 degrees for 5-8 minutes and watch them because you don't want them to burn. They are done when slightly golden on the edges.

Lemon Snow Bars
Recipe from Goldie Boyer (my Grammy)

Ingredients for crust:
½ cup butter
1 1/3 cups all-purpose flour
¼ cup sugar

Ingredients for filling:
2 eggs
¾ cup sugar
2 Tbsp all-purpose flour
¼ tsp baking powder
3 Tbsp lemon juice

Preheat oven to 350 degrees.

For Crust: Mix butter, flour and sugar. Pat into an 8X8 ungreased pan. Bake crust for 15-20 minutes.

Prepare filling by blending the ingredients for the filling together.

Pour the filling over the crust. Return to the oven and bake for 20 minutes. Sprinkle the top with confectioners' sugar while it is cooling. This dessert is best served cold.

Lunchroom Brownies

Mix together:
½ cup butter, softened
¼ cup cocoa powder
1 cup flour
1 cup sugar
2 eggs
2 tsp vanilla
½ cup chopped nuts

Preheat oven to 350 degrees. Mix all of the ingredients and put them in a greased square pan. Bake for 20-25 minutes. While they are cooking, prepare icing.

For the icing, mix together:
2 Tbsp butter
2 Tbsp milk
2 Tbsp cocoa
1 ½ cup powdered sugar
Pinch of salt

Peanut Butter Cookies

Ingredients:
½ cup butter, softened
½ cup peanut butter
½ cup brown sugar
½ cup sugar
1 egg
1 tsp vanilla
¼ tsp salt
1 ½ cups flour
1 tsp baking soda
1 bag of Hershey's kisses

Beat butter, peanut butter, sugar, egg, vanilla, and salt. Add flour and baking soda. Mix well. Shape into balls about a teaspoon size. Press a Hershey's kiss into each cookie. Bake at 375 degrees for 10-12 minutes.

Pecan Pie

Ingredients:
½ cup corn syrup
½ cup maple syrup
3 eggs
1 cup sugar
2 Tbsp butter, melted
1 tsp vanilla extract
1 ½ cups (6oz) coarsely chopped pecans (my mother in-law supplies me with pecans from Alabama and they are superior quality)
1 (9 inch) unbaked pie crust

Preheat oven to 350 degrees. Mix the corn syrup, maple syrup, eggs, sugar, butter and vanilla. Stir in the pecans. Pour the mixture into the pie crust. Bake on center rack for 60-70 minutes. Cool for at least two hours on a wire rack before serving.

Pecan Rolls

Recipe from Uncle Danny Holton who made this recipe over the years. The original recipe is from my Great, Great Grandmother Holton)

Ingredients:
5 cups chopped pecans
1 can Sweetened Condensed milk
1 lb. finely chopped dates
2 tsp water (to rinse can)
1 lb. box vanilla wafers, crushed
Powdered sugar to dust

Mix all ingredients well. I use a food processor to chop everything really fine. Divide into five rolls. Using wax paper with powdered sugar, roll into long logs. Refrigerate 2-3 hours.

Pie Crust

Ingredients:
2 cups flour
1 stick refrigerated butter
3 pinches of Kosher salt
¼ cup sugar
3 Tbsp cold water

Combine in food processor and blend until combined. Press into pie pan. This makes enough for two pies or one bottom and one top.

Poppy Seed Cake
(from Aunt Betty Stenack)

Ingredients:
1 cup butter (2 sticks)
1 ½ cups sugar
4 eggs divided (save the whites for later)
1 can or jar of poppy seeds
½ pint sour cream
2 cups flour
1 tsp. baking soda
½ tsp. salt
1 tsp. vanilla

Mix all of these ingredients together, except the egg whites.
Beat the egg whites. Fold into the batter. Pour into a greased
and floured Bundt pan.
Bake 350 degrees for 1 hour.

Pound Cake
From the old Holton Family Cookbook

RECIPE FOR: Pound Cake
SOURCE: Grandmama Lanier
PREPARATION TIME: _____ SERVINGS: _____

8 eggs separated
2 2/3 C. Sugar
8 T Cream
3 1/2 C Flour
1 tsp. Vanilla
1 lb. Margarine

Beat egg whites adding 1 tsp. Sugar.
Refridgerate.

Cream butter & sugar. Add egg
yolks 2 at a time. Add Flour &
cream alternating. Add Vanilla.
Fold in egg whites slowly & beat
until smooth.
Bake at 325° for 1 1/2 hours.

Pumpkin Crisp
From my dear college roommate Eva Gibson

Ingredients:
1 16oz can pumpkin
1 12oz can evaporated milk
1 cup sugar
3 eggs
2 sticks butter
1 box yellow cake mix
1 ½ cups chopped pecans
1 tsp vanilla extract
½ tsp cinnamon

Directions:
Preheat oven to 350 degrees. Beat eggs and mix in the pumpkin, vanilla, evaporated milk, sugar, and cinnamon. Pour into a greased 9X13 pan. Shake the dry cake mix over the mixture and pat gently, making sure the cake dust goes to the edges of the pan. Sprinkle the pecans over the top of the cake dust. Melt the butter and pour it over the top to soak the mix. Bake for 50 minutes, watching carefully at the end to make sure the nuts don't burn. Serve with whipped cream.

Pumpkin Pie

Ingredients:
¾ cup sugar
½ tsp salt
1 tsp ground cinnamon
½ tsp ground ginger
¼ tsp ground cloves
2 eggs
1 can pumpkin or 15oz of fresh cooked pumpkin
1 12 oz can evaporated milk
1 prepared pie crust

Directions:
Mix together the sugar, salt, cinnamon, ginger and cloves in a small bowl. Beat eggs in a large bowl. Stir in the pumpkin and the sugar-spice mixture. Gradually stir in the evaporated milk. Pour into the prepared pie shell. Bake in a preheated 425-degree oven for 15 minutes. Reduce temperature to 350 degrees. Bake 40-50 minutes or until knife inserted near the center comes out clean. Refrigerate overnight before serving.

If you are using fresh pumpkin, roast it as follows:
Heat oven to 400 degrees. Chop pumpkin in half and scoop out the seeds and fibers with a metal spoon. Discard the insides and sprinkle the insides of the pumpkin with salt. Lay the halves, flesh side down, on a sheet pan lined with parchment paper. Cook for 30-45 minutes. Remove from the pan and cool for one hour. Place in food processor until smooth (about 3 minutes). Store in the refrigerator for up to one week.

Ricotta Cake
Recipe from Zoe

Ingredients:
1 Yellow cake mix
3 Cups ricotta
¾ cup sugar
2 eggs
1 ½ tsp vanilla
Mixture of ¼ cup sugar and 2 tsp cinnamon for topping

Prepare the yellow cake mix with instructions on the box. Pour it into a greased and floured 13X9X2 pan.

In a separate bowl, mix together ricotta, sugar, eggs, and vanilla.

Pour the ricotta mixture slowly into the center of batter. Do not mix or touch.

Bake at 350 degrees for 40 minutes.

Remove from the oven and sprinkle the top with the sugar/cinnamon mixture. Return to the oven and bake another 30 minutes.

Rum Cake

Recipe from my Mema, Dorothy Holton

Ingredients:
1 18 ½ oz. yellow cake mix
1 3 ¾ oz. pack instant vanilla pudding
4 eggs
½ cup cold water
½ cup oil
½ cup Bacardi Dark Rum
1 cup chopped nuts (pecans or walnuts)
¼ lb. butter
¼ cup water
1 cup sugar

Preheat oven to 325 degrees. Grease and flour a 10" tube or 12 cup bunt pan. Sprinkle 1 cup chopped pecans or walnuts on the bottom of the pan.

Mix the yellow cake mix, vanilla pudding, eggs, ½ cup water, and oil together. Pour batter over nuts in the pan. Bake for 1 hour. Cool and then invert on your serving plate. Prepare the glaze by melting the butter, sugar, and ¼ cup water in a saucepan. Bring to a boil for five minutes stirring frequently. Remove from heat. Cool slightly. Add ½ cup Bacardi Rum. Stir.

Prick the top of the cake, drizzle and smooth glaze evenly and over the sides. Allow cake to absorb the glaze. Repeat until the glaze is used up.

Optional: decorate with whole cherries and boarder with frosting, whipped cream or powdered sugar.

Sand Tarts
From the old Holton Family Cookbook

RECIPE FOR: Sand Tarts

SOURCE: Mary Lee Dill

PREPARATION TIME: _____ SERVINGS: _____

1 C butter
1 C Pecans (finely chopped)
10 T Sugar
2 C Flour
1 T Vanilla

Mix all ingredients.
Bake at 350° on
Greased Cookie Sheet
for 10-12 minutes.
Dip in Powdered Sugar

Silver Moon Chocolate Chip Cookies
Recipe from my dear friend Wendy Avery

Ingredients:
2 ½ sticks unsalted butter, softened
½ cup sugar
½ cup packed dark brown sugar
1 tsp salt
1 large egg
2 tsp vanilla
2 cups all-purpose flour
2-3 cups semi-sweet chocolate chips

Beat together butter, sugars, and salt for about two minutes. Beat in egg and vanilla until combined, then reduce speed to low and mix in four until just combined. Fold in chocolate chips and chill, covered, at least four hours or overnight.

Preheat oven to 350 degrees. Drop 2 Tbsp mounds of dough about two inches apart onto an ungreased baking sheet. Bake about 10-15 minutes.

Sugar Cookies

Ingredients:
1 stick plus 2 Tbsp butter
1/3 cup sugar
1 cup flour
sprinkles

Preheat oven to 325 degrees. Cream the sugar and butter and then add the flour. Roll out dough, cut into shapes and place on an ungreased pan. Appy the sprinkles generously. Bake for 15-17 minutes.

DRINKS/COCKTAILS

Blue Hawaii

Combine Ingredients:
¾ oz Blue Curacao
1 ¼ oz Malibu Rum

Pour over ice.

Fill the rest of the 8oz glass with pineapple juice

Bucky's Mint Julep
Borrowed from the Grand Hotel for Andrew

Ingredients:
6 fresh mint leaves
1/8 tsp simple syrup
1 ¾ oz bourbon (Walker's Deluxe)
1 sprig mint leaf, sprinkled with powdered sugar
1 Maraschino cherry

Place mint leaves in 12-oz glass with Simple Syrup and a small amount of crushed ice. Muddle the ingredients in the bottom of the glass. Add crushed ice until half full. Then add bourbon. Continue to muddle ingredients and add ice until the glass is almost full and ice is pale green.

Garnish with powdered mint leaf (sprinkle powdered sugar over dampened leaf) and a maraschino cherry. Add a straw and serve.

Chai Tea

Ingredients:
2 black tea bags
2/3 cup water
½ cup soy milk
1 cardamom pod, crushed
3 slices of ginger
1 tsp sugar

Boil the water with the tea bags, cardamom pod and ginger for about five minutes. Stir in the sugar and the soy milk. Strain into cup.

Lychee Cocktails
Reminiscent of our trip to Disney World

Ingredients:
5 cups water
¾ cup sugar
1 cup lemon juice (about four lemons)
1 cup Malibu run
14 oz Lychee in a light syrup
ice

In a saucepan, bring to boil 1 cup water and sugar, stirring until sugar is dissolved. Pour into a pitcher. Add lemon juice, rum, lychees and their syrup. Put in the refrigerator and chill. Serve over ice.

Mojito

Ingredients:
3 tsp sugar
½ lime, juiced
¼ cup fresh mint leaves
1 oz white rum
Soda water

Put the sugar and lime juice in a glass. Crush a few fresh mint leaves into the sugar and lime juice. Add one ounce of white rum and ice cubes. Fill with soda water and serve with a sprig of mint.

St. Germaine Cocktail
Andrew and I discovered this recipe at Trio in Jackson

Combine Ingredients:
2 parts grapefruit
1-part gin
½ part St. Germaine
Sprigs of rosemary

Shake with rosemary and pour over ice with fresh sprig of rosemary in glass.

Grocery list that I use to restock the kitchen after a trip

Broccoli
Carrots
Mangos
Mushrooms
Potatoes
Scallions, or green onions
Spinach leaves
Star fruit
Tomatoes
Yellow onions
Zucchini/Yellow squash
Distilled Water
Juices
Flour tortilla shells
Jar of marinara sauce
Noodles/pasta
Instant oatmeal
Life cereal
Tea bags
Ground beef
Whole chicken
Can of chicken soup
Canned tomato paste
Canned tomato sauce
Rice-a-roni, one box
White rice, one bag
All-purpose flour
Olive oil
Salt
Aluminum foil
Napkins
Butter
Milk
Mozzarella cheese
Bagels or fresh bread
English muffins

Helpful tips that all cooks could benefit from:

1. Never measure over the bowl that you are adding ingredients to.
2. After baking a cake or other pastry, wait until it cools completely before trying to remove it from the pan.
3. If a recipe calls for minced garlic or ginger, use a micro plane to easily get the ingredient to the right consistency.
4. When a recipe calls for water, sometimes it can make a significant difference to substitute stock (chicken, beef, vegetable). It could make the recipe more flavorful, but be careful of the salt content of the recipe, because you don't want to make the dish too salty.
5. Three teaspoons are equal to one tablespoon
6. You can use ¼ cup canned pumpkin to replace an egg (if you are out of eggs), or ½ cup canned pumpkin to replace ½ cup oil, or ¾ cup canned pumpkin to replace 1 cup butter.
7. If you are cooking a dish in the oven that might spill over during the cooking process, put a separate pan on the rack underneath it to catch any drips.
8. You can substitute half and half for canned evaporated milk.
9. If the recipe calls for salt and pepper, add a small amount of salt and pepper at each addition to the recipe.
10. Keep powdered milk on hand just in case you run out of milk. Powdered milk is also a good addition to beauty face masks.

Dinner Ideas

*Chicken marinated in Italian dressing grilled on a grill press served with cous-cous and okra.
*Big salad with ham & cheese
*Baked chicken with rice, gravy and broccoli
*Beef roast with vegetables and rice
*Spaghetti with angel hair pasta
*Smokey pork chops with sweet potato and green beans with lemon
*Meatloaf with stuffing and carrots boiled in chicken broth
*Beef bourguignon over oven roasted new potatoes, served with steamed green beans and lemon
*Mesquite turkey, provolone and tomato sandwich, grilled, served with pumpkin soup
*Greek pizzas (mozzarella, tomato, olives, spinach, and feta)
Enchiladas
*Meatloaf, split pea soup, and little roasted potatoes
*Short ribs with mashed potatoes and green peas
*Gumbo with rice served with corn boiled in crawfish seasoning, with pan sautéed okra served on top of the gumbo
*Chicken chipotle tacos, heart of palm salad and yucca fries
*Mississippi mud roast with mashed potatoes and green beans
*BBQ chicken sandwiches with chips
*Grilled kabobs with curry yogurt sauce
*Chicken fricassee with yellow rice and grilled peppers
*Charcuterie board with meats, cheeses, berries, nuts, and olives
*Jerk shrimp with Caribbean potato soup
*Ham, stuffing, and green beans

Made in the USA
Middletown, DE
16 June 2023

32725091R00089